# A Young Person's Guide to the Beach

## for the beach-loving student

Gilbert Newton

# Dedication

This book is dedicated
to all my students –
past, present, and future.

Published by Gilbert Newton
gdnewton@comcast.net

Copyright 2024 by Gilbert Newton
All rights reserved.
Published in the United States 2024

ISBN 978-1-7328701-9-2

This book produced by Nancy Viall Shoemaker, West Barnstable Press

# TABLE OF CONTENTS

| | |
|---|---|
| Introduction . . . . . . . . . . . . . . . . . 1 | Jingle Shell . . . . . . . . . . . . . . . . . 34 |
| Materials needed . . . . . . . . . . . . 2 | Moon Snail . . . . . . . . . . . . . . . . . 36 |
| A few beachcombing rules . . . . . . . 3 | Mussels . . . . . . . . . . . . . . . . . . . 38 |
| Irish Moss . . . . . . . . . . . . . . . . . 4 | Oysters . . . . . . . . . . . . . . . . . . . 40 |
| Oyster Thief . . . . . . . . . . . . . . . 6 | Periwinkle Snail . . . . . . . . . . . . 42 |
| Rockweed . . . . . . . . . . . . . . . . . 8 | Quahog . . . . . . . . . . . . . . . . . . . 44 |
| Sea Lettuce . . . . . . . . . . . . . . . 10 | Razor Clam . . . . . . . . . . . . . . . . 46 |
| Cordgrass . . . . . . . . . . . . . . . . 12 | Sea Star . . . . . . . . . . . . . . . . . . 48 |
| Eelgrass . . . . . . . . . . . . . . . . . 14 | Slipper Snail . . . . . . . . . . . . . . . 50 |
| Barnacles . . . . . . . . . . . . . . . . 16 | Spider Crab . . . . . . . . . . . . . . . 52 |
| Bay Scallop . . . . . . . . . . . . . . . 18 | Sponges . . . . . . . . . . . . . . . . . . 54 |
| Blue Crab . . . . . . . . . . . . . . . . 20 | Tube Worms . . . . . . . . . . . . . . . 56 |
| Common Tern . . . . . . . . . . . . . 22 | Whelks . . . . . . . . . . . . . . . . . . . 58 |
| Fiddler Crab . . . . . . . . . . . . . . 24 | Glossary . . . . . . . . . . . . . . . . . . 60 |
| Green Crab . . . . . . . . . . . . . . . 26 | Scientific Names . . . . . . . . . . . . 62 |
| Hermit Crab . . . . . . . . . . . . . . 28 | About the Author . . . . . . . . . . . 64 |
| Herring Gull . . . . . . . . . . . . . . 30 | Acknowledgements . . . . . . . . . . 65 |
| Horseshoe Crab . . . . . . . . . . . . 32 | Books by Gilbert Newton . . . . . . 66 |

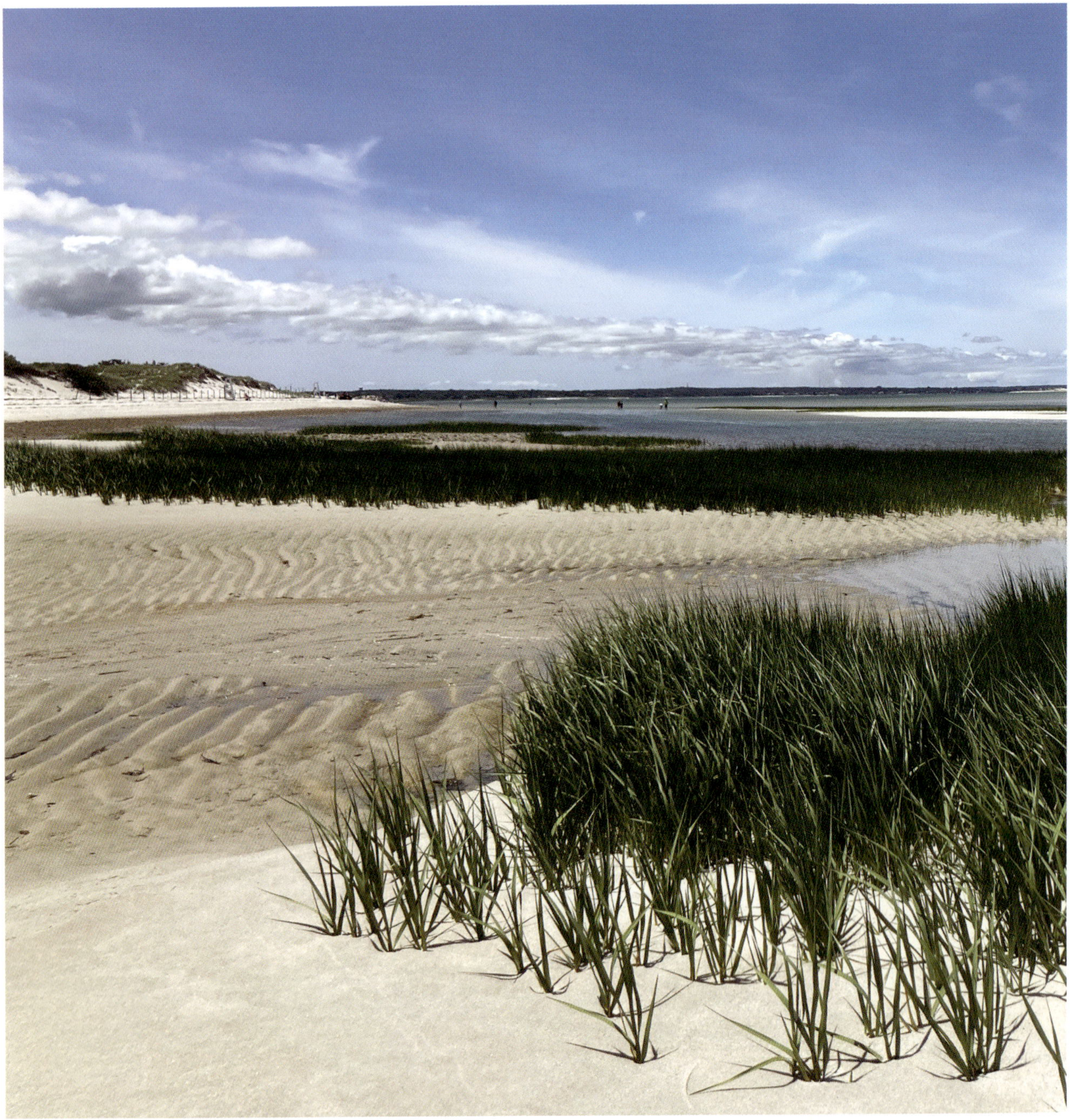

# Introduction

When I was a kid living on Cape Cod, I loved going to the beach to see what I could find. Every day was a new adventure where I could examine many seashore treasures. I remember collecting dozens of shells, starfish, and crabs. I knew even then at a young age that I wanted to be a marine biologist.

My collection became one large puzzle. What were the names of the critters I found? Where did they live? What did they feed on? How did they survive at the beach?

These and other questions filled my thoughts and imagination. And today I am still exploring the shoreline on Cape Cod and am always excited to see what I can find.

I hope that you can also experience the fun, joy, and pleasure of discovering life on the beach. Use this field guide to familiarize yourself with some of the common plants and animals that live on the ocean's edge. You may learn that this will turn into a lifetime experience and passion.

**Gil Newton**

# Materials needed as you get ready to explore!

1. A bucket and a tray for collecting
2. A hand lens (5x or 10x)
3. A ruler or measuring tape
4. A notebook and pencil
5. A dip net for collecting
6. Water shoes or boots
7. Sunscreen lotion and insect/tick repellent
8. Protective clothing for variations in weather

## While beachcombing can be done at any time of the year, certain precautions and planning should always be considered.

1. Children should be accompanied by an adult.
2. Observe all property rights. Obey "No Trespassing" signs.
3. If collecting and observing any live animals, return them to the same location.
4. Be careful when walking on rocks or jetties. They can be very slippery.
5. Strong surf and currents should be avoided.
6. Wear water shoes or boots to avoid cuts by broken glass or sharp shells and rocks.
7. Be mindful of areas with a large tidal range. Don't get stranded by a fast-moving high tide!
8. Be aware of any local laws that restrict access or activities such as collecting. Digging for shellfish may require a permit even if you are not keeping the shellfish.
9. Adults should be familiar with any parking regulations. Some places have seasonal parking fees or require passes.
10. Don't trample any coastal plants that are important for erosion control and for wildlife habitat.

## Let's go to the beach . . .

ALGAE

Irish Moss

4

# Irish Moss

Irish moss is a common red alga that is widely used as a food source and in many commercial products.

This seaweed is a deeply red to purple color with many flat blades up to four inches long.

Sometimes you will find that it is completely white.

That's because long exposure to the sun will bleach out the pigments responsible for its color.

ALGAE

**Oyster Thief**

# Oyster Thief

This green seaweed is very common on the beach and is also called green fleece. It has a spongy texture, and its branches have puffy, swollen tips. It can grow up to three feet in length, but frequently forms large mats.

The oyster thief prefers cold water, and can be a major pest in shellfish beds. It attaches to the shells of oysters, scallops, and slipper snails, weighing them down, and sometimes covering their filter-feeding siphon. This seaweed is invasive and difficult to control.

ALGAE

**Rockweed**

8

# Rockweed

Rockweed is a common brown alga that has a strong root-like holdfast which attaches to a rock jetty or on the edges of a salt marsh. Two opposite air bladders enable this seaweed to float to the surface of the water.

Rockweed is important as a shelter for some small animals such as periwinkle snails. In salt marshes rockweed can cover large clumps of ribbed mussels.

*Yes, that's a mussel hanging out with the rockweed!*

ALGAE

# Sea Lettuce

10

# Sea Lettuce

Sea lettuce gets its name because it looks a lot like garden lettuce.

Sea lettuce consists of large green sheets that often fold along the edges.

Sea lettuce can grow up to three feet long. While it usually grows along the edge of the seashore, it can be very abundant in polluted bays and estuaries.

Sea lettuce is edible and is used in soups and seaweed salads.

**PLANTS**

# Cordgrass

12

# Cordgrass

Cordgrass is a tall grass that grows in a salt marsh where the water meets the land. It can survive coverage by the salt water during high tides and strong coastal storms. Cordgrass protects the coast from erosion.

When it dies, it forms large mats that get washed out to sea and consumed by many small animals and bacteria. Cordgrass survives in this salty environment by releasing the salt through its leaves.

**PLANTS**

**Eelgrass**

14

# Eelgrass

Eelgrass is one of the few true plants in the ocean. It has leaves, stems, roots, flowers, fruits, and seeds. It spreads by an underground stem called a rhizome.

You may find it along the beach in large mats. The green leaves are long and grass-like and become entangled with the seaweed on shore.

Many animals, such as scallops and blue crabs, depend on the thick eelgrass beds for shelter and food. If you look closely, you may find several small animals and algae attached to the eelgrass.

ANIMALS

# Barnacles

16

# Barnacles

Barnacles are attached to rocks, pilings, and even other animals such as horseshoe crabs or spider crabs. Like many other marine animals, the young larval stage of this crustacean is part of the floating plankton. After the larvae settle on a hard surface such as a rock jetty, the adult will grow up to one inch long.

These animals are filter-feeders, using their tiny feet to capture small particles of food while waving through the water.

If they are attached to a moving crab, they get transported to various locations where food is available. Barnacles can also form distinct bands or zones along a jetty or piling, and are often found near a population of rockweed.

ANIMALS

**Bay Scallop**

18

# Bay Scallop

Bay scallops are clams that do not burrow in the sand, but move by snapping their two shells together.

They are found in eelgrass habitats and can grow up to three inches long.

The shell has distinct ribs along the outside. They don't have a long life cycle, only living up to two years. Sometimes large numbers of scallops wash up on the beach after a storm.

ANIMALS

Blue Crab

20

GNN

# Blue Crab

The blue crab is a common species that is easy to identify with its blue shell and legs. The hind legs are shaped like a paddle and enable it to swim.

There are nine spines or teeth along each margin of the shell. The blue crab is very aggressive and can pinch, so it should be handled only with a net. It feeds on other crabs and small fish, and is a food source for birds.

These animals grow by molting, the shedding of the shell. They also have a strong ability to grow lost claws – a process called regeneration.

ANIMALS

# Common Tern

22

# Common Tern

Common terns are frequently seen near gull populations. They can be identified by their forked tails, black caps, and orange bill.

These animals are excellent "fishermen" and can be observed diving in the water for small fish such as the silverside minnow.

They are very protective of their nesting sites in the dunes and will respond noisily to any intruders.

In Massachusetts the common tern is listed as a species of special concern.

ANIMALS

# Fiddler Crab

24

# Fiddler Crab

Fiddler crabs are abundant in the salt marsh. They live in underground burrows in large numbers.

The male fiddler crab has one large claw which is used in defense and courtship.

Fiddler crabs are an important food source for birds and larger crabs.

Their burrows help aerate the marsh, and their wastes help fertilize the soil.

ANIMALS

## Green Crab

26

# Green Crab

An abundant animal living under rocks and jetties is the green crab. This animal was introduced from Europe and has become very invasive.

Green crabs have pointed hind legs and can grow up to three inches long. There are five teeth or spines along the margin and three in the front of the shell. Green crabs feed on other animals in the sediments such as clams and worms.

At right: a green crab feeding on a skate.

ANIMALS

Hermit Crab

28

# Hermit Crab

Sometimes you may see a small snail moving a lot faster than the others. Take a closer look and you will discover that a tiny hermit crab has taken up residence in the snail shell.

If you hold it quietly in your hand, it will emerge, and you may observe its large right claw. Hermit crabs must change shells as they grow larger, though this common small species doesn't grow more than a half inch long.

ANIMALS

# Herring Gull

30

# Herring Gull

The term "seagulls" includes several different species of gulls. The most common is the herring gull, an abundant scavenger that feeds on mollusks, crabs, and all the food garbage left by people.

The herring gull can grow over two feet tall and has black tips on the wings. This animal is overpopulated in many areas and is very competitive with other species, including many endangered birds.

ANIMALS

**Horseshoe Crab**

32

# Horseshoe Crab

A horseshoe crab is a primitive animal that evolved over 400 million years ago. It is not a true crab, but is more closely related to ancient spiders and scorpions.

A horseshoe crab is harmless; you can pick one up by lifting it underneath the animal. But don't pick it up by the tail. That can harm the animal! It uses its tail to right itself if upside down.

A horseshoe crab has 10 eyes. A pair of compound eyes are visible on the front of the shell. This animal also has blue blood which contains a substance that is widely used in testing medical equipment and vaccines for their safety.

Horseshoe crabs eat clams and worms. When the animal gets too big for its shell, it grows another and leaves a molt behind on the beach.

ANIMALS

## Jingle Shell

34

# Jingle Shell

One of the prettiest clams on the beach is the jingle shell.

Shells can be yellow (the most common), orange, or silvery gray. The two halves of the shell are not even. The lower half is flat with a small hole in it.

These animals are sometimes called toenail shells or mermaid's toenails. Many people like to collect them and make necklaces and other jewelry.

ANIMALS

**Moon Snail**

36

# Moon Snail

Moon snails are carnivorous. They like to eat clams and oysters. They can do a great deal of damage to a clam bed. After drilling a hole in a clam shell, they feed on the clam using a structure called a radula. Moon snails can eat several clams each day.

They also have a large foot for burrowing in the sand where they leave trails that can be seen at low tide. Sometimes you can find their egg masses in a circular sandy structure called a sand collar.

ANIMALS

**Mussels**

38

# Mussels (Blue & Ribbed)

Blue mussels are characterized by a long blue shell that can grow three to six inches long. They can be quite abundant along beaches with rock jetties and other hard structures. They use a structure called a siphon to filter small bits of food, such as algae, out of the water. They attach themselves to a substrate with strong byssal threads.

Ribbed mussels (at right) have shells with ridges or ribs along their length. They are also filter-feeders and grow in large clumps around the banks of salt marshes. Ribbed mussels are often covered by a clump of rockweed which protects them from the sun and predators.

**ANIMALS**

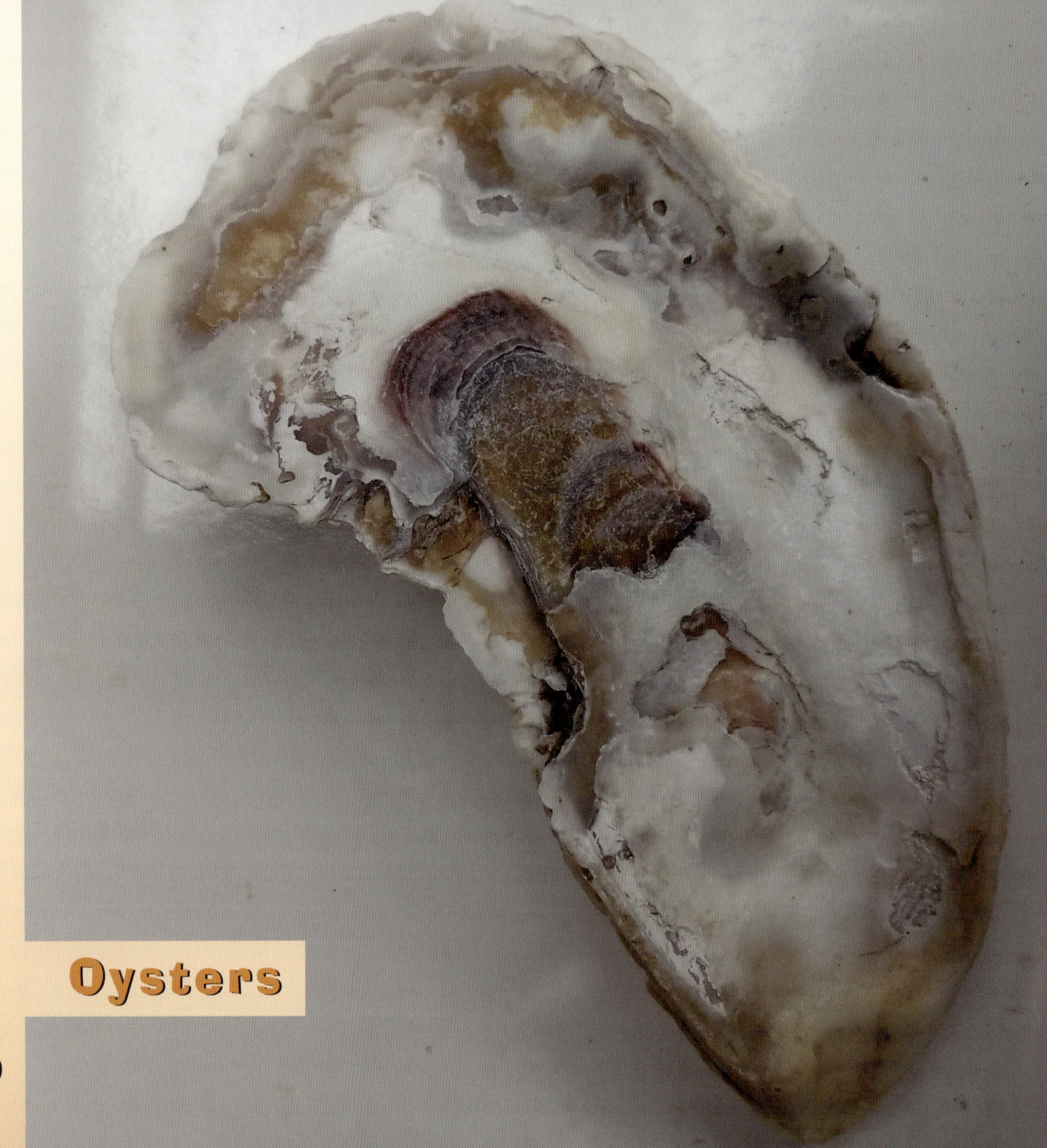

**Oysters**

40

# Oysters

A very productive and commercially important mollusk is the oyster. An oyster can spawn several times a summer and in the process release millions of eggs. After fertilization the young larvae settle on a hard surface where they remain for the rest of their lives.

Oysters have irregular shaped shells and are often found growing in clumps on older shells in an oyster bed.

ANIMALS

**Periwinkle Snail**

42

# Periwinkle Snail

The common periwinkle snail is found mainly along a rock jetty at the beach. This tiny snail grows to a little over one inch long. Its shell is dark and spiral. The periwinkle feeds mainly on tiny algae that it scrapes from the rocks using its radula.

This snail can live for long periods of time outside the water. It can also be found throughout the year.

ANIMALS

**Quahog**

# Quahog

The shell of the quahog is thick and oval-shaped, looking somewhat like a heart. There is often a purple coating on the inside of the shell.

Quahogs can grow up to three inches or more and can live as long as two decades. You can determine the age of a quahog by counting the thick bands on the shell. Each one represents one year of growth. This can be a fun activity, as you compare the size of the animal with its approximate age.

ANIMALS

Razor Clam

46

# Razor Clam

Razor clams prefer a muddy open area. They burrow under the surface of the mud flat that may be part of a beach system or salt marsh. They use their strong foot to dig very quickly in the mud.

It is more likely that you will find a shell on the surface. The shell is about five times longer than it is wide and brown along the edges. This animal is sometimes called the jackknife clam because of its shape.

ANIMALS

Sea Star

48

# Sea Star

Sea stars are found in tide pools or in the crevices of rock jetties. Sea stars love to feed on mussels. Their arms attach to the mussel, pry it open, and slide their stomach inside the mussel to digest it. If a sea star loses an arm, it can grow or regenerate a new one. Sea stars move slowly with small tube feet that grip the surface like tiny suction cups. Sea stars are related to sea urchins, sand dollars, and sea cucumbers.

ANIMALS

**Slipper Snail**

50

# Slipper Snail

The slipper snail is a common mollusk that is often washed up on sandy beaches in huge numbers. Many of them can be found in stacks, or attached to other shells, rocks, and seaweed. They are easily identified by a small flat structure that looks like a platform along the opening of the shell. The shell may grow around an inch in size, with the females being slightly larger than the males.

ANIMALS

# Spider Crab

# Spider Crab

Look carefully to find a spider crab because this animal is an expert at camouflage. The spider crab has a brown, spiny carapace or shell that helps it blend in with the muddy substrate.

The animal grows to about four inches in length, but its legs can extend up to a foot. This animal is harmless and feeds mainly on bits of organic material in the water and sediments. It can also enhance its camouflage by attaching algae and small animals to its shell.

ANIMALS

Sponges

54

# Sponges

Sponges are simple primitive animals. They have no organs or organ systems. Their bodies are composed of three layers. One layer contains collar cells which beat the water, setting up small currents that flow into the sponge through tiny pores. As filter-feeders, they trap small particles of food for digestion. A common species is the red beard sponge. When alive this animal is bright red with many branches. However, it quickly loses its color after it dies and turns brown.

ANIMALS

## Tube Worms

56

# Tube Worms

You may find a shell that has some hard, squiggly-shaped structures attached to it. These are the casings of a tube worm. The animals will not be present if the shell has washed up on the beach. The live animal feeds on plankton using its feathery tentacles and can grow up to three inches long. Its casings are made of calcium carbonate (lime) just like the shell of the mollusk that it is attached to.

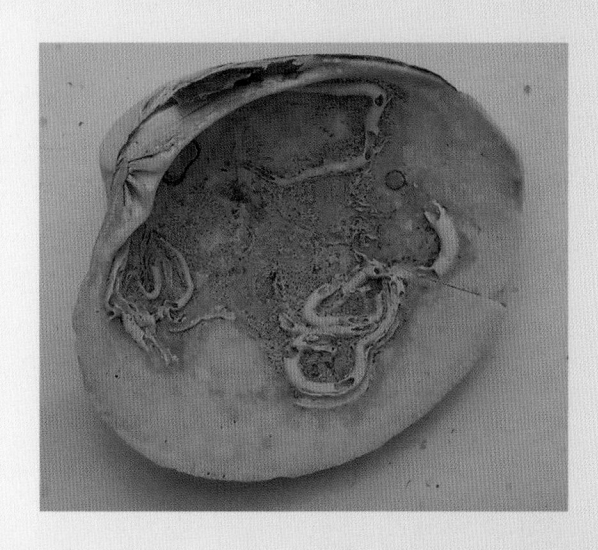

ANIMALS

# Whelks

58

# Whelks

## (Knobbed and Channeled)

Two of the largest snails are the knobbed (at left) and the channeled (at right) whelks. Their major difference is that the knobbed whelk has bumps or knobs on the outer shell.

These are carnivorous animals and use a radula to feed on their prey. Occasionally you can find their brown egg cases. Each capsule contains several young whelks. If there are two conspicuous edges on each disk-shaped capsule, it's a knobbed whelk. If there is only one sharp edge, it's a channeled whelk.

# Scientific Names

## ALGAE

| | |
|---|---|
| Irish moss | *Chondrus crispus* |
| Oyster thief | *Codium fragile* |
| Rockweed | *Fucus vesiculosus* |
| Sea lettuce | *Ulva lactuca* |

## PLANTS

| | |
|---|---|
| Cordgrass | *Spartina alterniflora* |
| Eelgrass | *Zostera marina* |

## ANIMALS

| | |
|---|---|
| Barnacles | *Semibalanus balanoides* |
| Bay scallops | *Argopecten irradians* |
| Blue crab | *Callinectes sapidus* |
| Common tern | *Sterna hirundo* |
| Fiddler crabs | *Uca* species |
| Green crabs | *Carcinus maenas* |
| Herring Gull | *Larus smithsonianus* |

# SCIENTIFIC NAMES

## ANIMALS cont'd

| | |
|---|---|
| Horseshoe crab | *Limulus polyphemus* |
| Jingle shell | *Anomia simplex* |
| Moon snail | *Euspira heros* |
| Mussels (Ribbed) | *Geukensia demissa* |
| Mussels (Blue) | *Mytilus edulis* |
| Oysters | *Crassostrea virginica* |
| Periwinkle snails | *Littorina littorea* |
| Quahogs | *Mercenaria mercenaria* |
| Razor clams | *Ensis leei* |
| Sea stars | *Asterias rubens* |
| Slipper snails | *Crepidula fornicata* |
| Spider crab | *Libinia emarginata* |
| Sponges | *Microciona prolifera* (red beard sponge) |
| | *Haliclona oculata* (finger sponge) |
| Tube worms | *Spirorbis* species |
| | *Hydroides* species |
| Whelks | *Busycon carica* (knobbed whelk) |

## About the Author

Gilbert Newton, a Cape Cod native, taught environmental and marine science at Sandwich High School for nearly four decades. He has also been teaching at the Cape Cod Community College and the Massachusetts Maritime Academy for many years. His classes include coastal ecology, coastal zone management, ecological sustainability, and marine botany. In 2013 he became the first Director of the Sandwich STEM Academy. Gil has also taught for the Falmouth Academy, Bridgewater State University, and the Waquoit Bay National Estuarine Research Reserve. He was the Program Director for the Advanced Studies and Leadership Program (ASLP) at the Massachusetts Maritime Academy for 14 years. He has been the Education Director for Cape Cod Learning Tours.

One of the founders of the Barnstable Land Trust, Gil is past president of the Association to Preserve Cape Cod, and former chairman of the Barnstable Conservation Commission. He completed his graduate work in biology at Florida State University. Gil is the author of several books about the environment including the recent *The Sandy Beach*.

# Acknowledgements

Thank you to Nancy Viall Shoemaker for her photographs and continuing professional advice and guidance in the creation and design of all my books.

Thank you to Chris Dumas for generously providing his excellent photographs on pages 1, 7, 14, 15, 17, 19, 22-25, 27, 32, 37, 43, and 59.

Shellfish Biologist Elizabeth Lewis was the photographer of the oyster cluster.

The Association to Preserve Cape Cod graciously offered a photo of cordgrass.

A special thank you to Scott Prior, for giving us the beautiful image of his painting on the front cover.

# Books by Gilbert Newton

Seaweeds of Cape Cod Shores

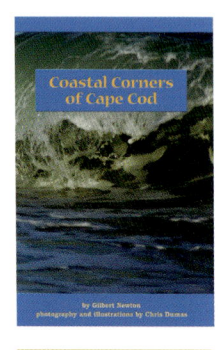

Coastal Corners of Cape Cod

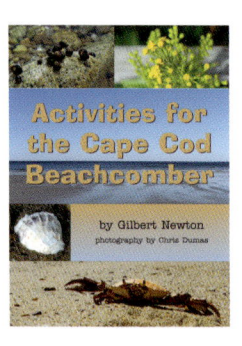

Activities for the Cape Cod Beachcomber

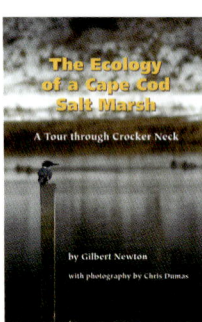

The Ecology of a Cape Cod Salt Marsh

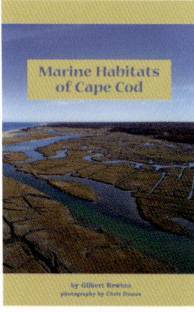

Marine Habitats of Cape Cod

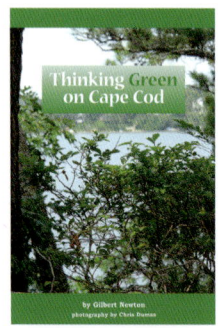

Thinking Green on Cape Cod

Discovering the Cape Cod Shoreline

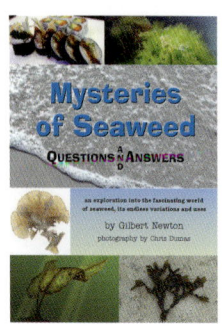

Mysteries of Seaweed: Questions and Answers

The Sandy Beach

All books are published by West Barnstable Press.

This book was designed and typeset by West Barnstable Press. The font used for the title and chapter heads is **Ad Lib**, designed by Freeman Craw in 1961. The text fonts used are **Frutiger** (designed in 1976 by Swiss typographer Adrian Frutiger) and American Typewriter (created by Joel Kaden and Tony Stan in 1974).

Printed on recycled paper